HOME DECORATION WITH A CHINESE FLAIR

HOME DECORATION WITH A CHINESE FLAIR

Text by Zhu Wen

Photographs by Liu Shenghui

Reader's Digest

The Reader's Digest Association, Inc.
Pleasantville, New York / Montreal / Sydney

FOR SHANGHAI PRESS & PUBLISHING DEVELOPMENT COMPANY
Managing Directors: Wang Youbu, Xu Naiqing
Editorial Director: Wu Ying
Editors: Yang Xiaohe, Yuan Yuan
Assistant Editor: Xu Xiaoyin

Text: Zhu Wen
Photographs: Liu Shenghui
Translators: He Jing, Amber Scorah

Interior and Cover Designer: Shenghui Studio

Library of Congress Cataloging-in-Publication Data
Wen, Zhu, 1978-
   Home decoration with a Chinese flair / Zhu Wen & Liu Shenghui.
         p. cm.
   ISBN 978-1-60652-048-2
1. Interior decoration–Chinese influences. I. Liu, Shenghui. II. Title.
NK2115.5.E84W46 2009
747–dc22

                                                             2009020742

FOR READER'S DIGEST
Executive Editor, Trade Publishing: Dolores York

THE READER'S DIGEST ASSOCIATION, INC.
President and Chief Executive Officer: Mary Berner
President of Asia Pacific: Paul Heath
President and Publisher, U.S. Trade Publishing: Harold Clarke

Printed in China by Shenzhen Donnelley Printing Co. Ltd.

1 3 5 7 9 10 8 6 4 2

CONTENTS

PROLOGUE

China may be a distant, unknown and perhaps somewhat mysterious country to you. Even so, you very likely have heard a lot about Ming furniture, Chinese cuisine and other representative symbols of Chinese culture. With its several-thousand-year heritage, the beauty of the culture shines forth in diverse forms, one being interior design. Following simplicity, pastoral lyricism and classicism of the Chinese style has become an influence on interior design worldwide. The mystique of the Orient evokes a-la-mode fashion and inspires designers. Chinese culture has become a source of creativity for designers.

A Western-style home adorned with well-chosen Chinese accents is sure to be uniquely beautiful. A balanced mixture of Western and Chinese styles, coupled with unexpected touches, will draw attention to the ingenuity of the designer. For example, thick and heavy oil paint can evoke the freshness and charm of lotus, simple black and white can set off the refinement of embroidery, and cool metallic finishes can tone down the heaviness of carved wood.

Want to add a unique Chinese touch to your home? There's no need to rack your brain or make a fuss. All you need to do is to simply apply some Chinese decorating techniques and add a few Chinese elements. A small corner can give off a lingering and rich Oriental charm. It may be in the living room, where two chairs sit in symmetry on both sides of a tea table, embodying the beauty of order long valued in China. Or, perhaps the bedroom, with a yarn drapery partition, emanating the spirit of traditional Chinese philosophy. Try mixing and matching to create a symphony of Western and Chinese elements, you will find that the graceful and flamboyant Rococo style and the Qing style with its gloss and gold have much in common; both Scandinavian hand-made furniture and Ming furniture showcase simple curved designs and natural textures. Let your imagination go, and you can transform modern materials and elements into replicas of Oriental beauty. Pieces of frosted glass with lights shining through, in meticulous display, are reminiscent of a Chinese-style panel; neat and simple wood furniture in the shape of the Chinese character *xi* supplies a festive and harmonious atmosphere with a splash of red.

A well-furnished home can have its atmosphere enhanced in a magical way by using a few exotic pieces of furniture or accessories. The simple Ming style, the imposing Qing style, humble bamboo, elegant jade, an elegant bonsai pot or a glittering palace lantern all reflect the diversity of the Chinese style, and are all capable of adding finesse to your home. In addition, a simple change of color may evoke the atmosphere of a Chinese painting—elegant lush green, rich red, and even black and white. These are all things reminiscent of a typical Chinese home.

A Western-style home adorned with Chinese accents will enhance your modern life.

CHAPTER ONE THE BEAUTY OF FORM IN CHINESE-STYLE FURNITURE

The key in creating a Chinese-style home lies in reproducing a Chinese atmosphere. However, the so-called "Chinese Style" is hard to define in a precise and accurate way. China is a sophisticated, multi-ethnic and multi-polar country, which is reserved and solemn, free and conceited; gentle and elegant, enchanting and flamboyant; simple and natural, meticulous and detailed. Thus, interior design with a Chinese flair is diverse and colorful. This article provides a comprehensive overview of this very style with the help of pictures. We introduce the art and rules of traditional Chinese decoration through an example of symmetrically arranged living rooms. A back room with a couch in the east and a table in the west is a true reflection of the art of prose writing; free in format but consistent in spirit. A boudoir decorated with layers of yarn drapery seethes with the emotion of a chanted poem and a hummed tune, performed amid fragrance and embroidered quilts. A study with bright windows, a clean desk, and a brush and ink tells stories of ancient scholars studying hard all year long; a bathroom with a blue-and-white porcelain washing basin reveals the romantic sentiment of the Chinese, which is deep and hidden, yet everywhere.

If you are interested in learning about the beauty of form in Chinese-style decorating, Chinese poetry is the right medium. The beauty of Chinese poetry lies in its ability to create a feeling of presence. It is lofty yet mild, indirect and logical, using simple words that carry great weight. Modern decorating places emphasis on comfort. Applying techniques and skills of traditional Chinese decoration by adding a few pieces of traditional Chinese furniture in certain rooms may be just enough to add a touch of Oriental mystique.

Refreshingly beautiful, Chinese elements have brought about a new trend in decorating circles around the globe.

LIVING ROOM

The oil painting is of modern style, and the chairs are trendy in both style and material. However, the classic layout and symbolic color scheme, along with the narrow rectangular table with its recessed legs, red candles and the Buddha, all tell anyone familiar with Chinese culture that this is the true style of this room. It is unmistakable.

A camphor chest with a piece of glass placed on top instantly becomes an exquisite tea table. Ornaments can be strategically placed on a flat-topped, narrow, recessed-leg table in a way that reflects the good taste of the owner. Two western-style sofas and an old Chinese narrow table sit harmoniously together, thanks to their similarly simple lines. Meanwhile, a blue-and-white porcelain vase is an arresting piece that can accentuate the overall style of the room.

The official hat chair is a typical piece of Ming furniture. It got its name because it resembles the hat of Chinese ancient officials. The two armchairs here have four protruding ends, being the top rail and arms. The classic traditional furniture is here arranged in a black-white-grey cold-feeling space with an industrial beauty. It is not unexpected at all. In fact, the furniture and the space set each other off very nicely.

Despite their modern design, the sofas echo the straight and simple lines of the tea table and the table-shaped cabinet. With its refined polished finish, the Chinese-style furniture retains its classic feel while simplifying its complexity. The traditionally-styled partition tempers the modern and avant-garde feel of the lamps and curtains. It is not possible to produce a feeling of Oriental mystique randomly. Rather, an effective design requires proper integration and much time and effort.

This design is based on the concept of "heritage and development": The layout of the cabinet, sofa, side chairs and television stand breaks away from tradition, forming two vertical axes of symmetry. A fresh feeling of mix and match is layered over a sober foundation. Likewise with the furniture design. The chair back looks like a comb. The cabinet lock is done in a simple and abstract form. Even the tea table looks like a long desk. The resulting effect is that Chinese heritage is balanced against a modern background.

A woven basket used to keep newspaper and books in adds a taste of Chinese style to the room. Nearby, several Chinese-style chairs and tables with beautiful and detailed carvings, coupled with a painting and some ornaments, make a fascinating focal point. You do not need to decorate every corner of the room, one focal point is enough.

Stone, used as either a wall material or for a fireplace, can create different effects. Lamps, whether classic or modern, show that beauty transcends cultural differences and national borders. But the essence of this room may be in the symmetry: the fresh flowers and bamboo, the comb backed chair and the glass table face each other. Furthermore, the television and the antithetical couplet on black wood are facing each other.

The splashes of Chinese red shape the style of this living room. The theme is repeated throughout in such an orderly way—in the sofas, tea table, lamp covers, and the colorful glass. The large blue-and-white porcelain vase, together with the other Chinese-style elements scattered throughout, is reminiscent of the sensational mix of Chinese and Western styles found in the Winter Palace, even though you are in a typical Western room.

The position of the old-style lounging chair and the carpet patterned with flowers and birds may seem casual, but it lightens up the would-be seriousness of the square space and traditional furniture. The opening in the wall and the calligraphy artwork are at different heights on the wall, yet balance each other. In addition, the freeform wood sculpture emerges as the focal point of the design. The orchid plant highlights the free and natural style of the room.

In addition to detailed carving and refined craftsmanship, traditional Chinese-style furniture has another side—that of being simple and natural. These tables and stools with their simple lines and lack of embellishment reflect the lofty sentiment of Chinese ancient literati who made light of money and enjoyed their poor but comfortable life. The specially designed lights create shadows of dancing branches on the light green wall, adding a touch of serenity and ingenuity to the room.

The red wall shines and contrasts with the gold-painted furniture, a true reflection of Chinese style. Several refined silk cushions on the simple sofa bed echo the glamour of the cabinet. The simple and unsophisticated blue stone floor and the small ceramic vase serve as a neutralizer, balancing the overall style.

A wide *kang* (heatable stone bed) table, a coal grate and a smoke hood, all surrounded by three sofas, are the center of the living room. This practical style is reminiscent of the smart and bold nomads that reside in Northern China. Several painted chests, with their red or flower patterns and their heaviness, balance the simple lines of the book shelf perfectly. The beauty of masculinity prevails in the air.

With its collection of trunks and cabinets in diverse styles, chairs and embroidered stools with different features, crocks and jars from ancient times, and an imported modern pendant lamp and fireplace, this space seems to tell a story about the 5000-year-old culture of China. It is "orderly in its disorder."

A sofa is more stately than a chair. It is deemed by the Chinese as the seat of honor when showing hospitality to guests. In this room, thick cushions are placed on the sofa. The antithetical couplet, which was traditionally placed on the front door of homes, now appears on the unique cabinet cover. Ancient maxims are applied to create a Chinese atmosphere.

This kind of sofa bed is also called a Buddha bed. Therefore, it is more than fitting to put a Buddha on the narrow kang table. Amid the dim lights, a wisp of fragrance fills the air. The other-worldly arc-shaped legs and outward curving apron of the furniture are strong characteristics of the Ming dynasty, thus the strong Chinese flavor.

Can you guess what is hidden inside the Chinese cabinet? It is a television set. This simple idea reconciles functionality with style. Plum cushions and ginger-yellow sofa covers indicate a traditional taste for beauty. The sofas act as the transition piece from the Chinese-style furniture to the Western Christmas tree.

Self-controlled and modest Chinese literati always aspired to live a free, detached and secluded life. Bamboo blinds, a traditional painted box, a mottled wooden box and a casual layout can give a room a touch of the natural. A bouquet of wild flowers seems to be smiling quietly.

In a home without many Chinese elements, following the conventional way of decorating is the key to create an atmosphere. In this room, the ceiling, together with a large landscape painting, form an axis that accentuates the symmetry of the space. Selecting dark, gold color along with the right furniture and decorations gives a feeling of splendor rather than luxury. The effect is an atmosphere reflecting the seriousness and grace of a Chinese-style living room.

In traditional Chinese architecture, a window is not only used for ventilation and sunlight. In effect, with the right design, it can act as the perfect picture frame for the scenery outside. Its fancy carvings showcase a special beauty of pattern. In a narrow and closed space, one can even put in an artificial window. It not only draws the mind to muse as to what is behind it, but also adds a small twist to a symmetrical and conventional layout, and can substitute for the usual art found on walls.

Perhaps at first glance, all you see here is just a modern room in black and white. But on closer examination, you will find that the standing lamp in the corner, the lines of the rails, the ceramic tomb figures, and the furniture in the dining room all have a strong Chinese flavor. The feeling is that of a typical home in Southern China.

Besides a typically-styled armchair with a curved seat, any side chair with arms can be used as an armchair. Put two armchairs together with a small square table, and obtain a classic symmetrical style. Its structure reflects the virtues and ethics of traditional Chinese culture. Hanging two scrolls on the wall draws attention to a door panel carved with flowers, which serves as a partition. The fine carving techniques complement the furniture and make the space feel larger.

An eight-immortal table and two master chairs with a long table behind reflect a typical living room layout. Despite the predictable layout, the flamboyant furniture adds drama to the simple and plain style. The distance between the small red cabinet on the table and the windows with carvings is an innovative touch. If you want something unusual in your everyday life, why not start with an unusual scene at home?

It looks like a back room where the hostess entertains her best girlfriends. The lights shine on the wall, setting a warm tone for private gossip. The simple and smooth lines and the tasteful design of the furniture sparkle with feminine beauty. The old-fashioned canopy bed covered with embroidered pillows adds a sense of intimacy and laziness.

Sometimes, your dream of enjoying an idle life can only be realized by having your own private corner. A sofa and several piles of books are enough. Loose bamboo blinds can give you privacy from the outside world. This kind of space keeps Buddha in your heart. Excellent interior design tells what kind of person the owner is, just like the heaven concealed inside a flower.

A row of tall red panels with carved patterns is prominent and sets the classic tone for this room. In contrast, the other pieces of furniture are much more understated. The wardrobe and the pot have simple lines and colors; the chairs and the flower stand together complement the overall style.

DINING ROOM

Thanks to its simple touches and tidy layout, this room is filled with the purity of the Zen spirit. The square lines of the painting table and the two ceramic vases placed at the corner mark the honest, straightforward character of the homeowner, while the curvy design of lamp-hanger chairs and the upright lotus leaves seem to indicate his easy-going and amicable personality.

In this room, the pendant lamp, the cabinet and the blue-and-white porcelain unite to set a Chinese tone. Even the set of Western tableware uses the color of Chinese red to underline the theme. Satin brocade cushions placed on modern chairs further accentuate the style. In addition, the patterns on the window frame and the red glass of the windows reiterate the main theme. Nothing is lacking.

This is a red world. You sit against red, see red and use red. Red is at your fingertips, in every corner and even above you, on the ceiling. There is red paper, fabric, paint, and wood; red tableware, lamps, and furniture. For the Chinese, red represents happiness, celebration, and luck. Red is the heart and the soul of this room, and very suitably, red is the nickname for China.

Comb backed chairs impart a fresh and natural flavor to this room. Coupled with the green plants and the outside scenery partially obscured by the bamboo blinds, a simple and deep impression is created. The bird cage hanging on the tree, the baskets casually scattered, and the oil-paper umbrella hidden in the corner give the dining room with a feeling of warmth, refinement and elegance. These are all typical characteristics of an average resident of Southern China.

Outside the moon-shaped window is a beautiful scene of green trees and lush leaves, which seems to be right on the axis. By incorporating the outside scenery, the interior atmosphere becomes more alive and inspirational. Chairs that look like meditation chairs, and the folding screen with images of beautiful ladies enhance the traditional appeal. The rose red of the cushions in contrast with the green outside represents a typical Chinese method of mixing and matching elements. This enables the indoors and the outdoors to brighten each other.

Despite featuring a mixture of many elements, this room follows quite a lot of conventional practices. Everywhere you look, the furniture, ornaments, and paintings are arranged in symmetry, uniting their different styles. The layout adheres to traditional Chinese principles, in which a stand is put against the wall under a mirror behind a table and vases are put on the stand. To truly capture an authentic Chinese flavor, you must first learn about Chinese culture.

The rawness of the wooden beams, wooden structure and the wooden floor are a perfect match for the stone carvings and wooden wall ornamentation. This extremely natural and simple feeling is in sharp contrast with the refinement evident in the steel-armed chairs and carved furniture. This type of contrast catches one's attention through its contradiction.

Thirty or forty years ago, when refrigerators were not yet popularly used in Southern China, this type of buffet with a screen door was widely found in ordinary homes. The porcelain jugs and large bowls placed on top of the buffet are reminiscent of times gone by. These antique items bring back memories, bringing about the realization that, although time flies, we are grounded in our past.

Despite its stark black-and-white color scheme and linear layout, this room still has a Chinese flavor, due to the table, chairs and ceramic tomb figurines. Even the glass lamp, with its strong industrial feel, is reminiscent of a traditional sunken panel.

The modern, milky-white curtain sways with the breeze, next to a wall painted in red like a palace. Western tableware is glinting on the traditional eight-immortal table. A chair of a different style sits serenely amongst its peers. The ancient door on the wall symbolizes sharing and communication, transcends time and finds consensus within the differences.

Old Shanghai is a special element of Chinese style, as it derives from the cultural blend of the West and China. The furniture, for example, combines Chinese materials and colors with Western styles. Traditional carving techniques are used along with foam cushions, demonstrating a people-oriented philosophy. But in essence, it is still a Chinese style, and evokes memories of the formal attire of a 1930s Shanghainese woman—her slender and delicate *qipao* (cheongsam) hidden inside a Western overcoat.

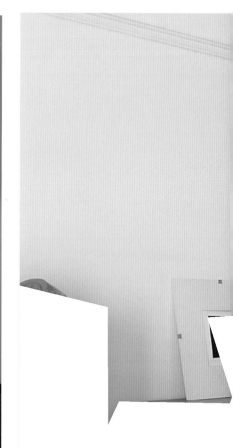

Glass, mirror and stainless steel have an industrial flavor; while the timber, porcelain and bamboo leaves add a living touch. It is like the contrary and complementary relationship between black and white. If tastefully combined, a beautiful room design results.

A big red cabinet stands against a light green wall. Only Fauvism dares to use such bold colors. Blossoming flowers on rural fabrics purvey the good wishes of the owner. In such modern atmosphere, the transparent chairs at the center of the table feel natural. The Chinese style shows its passion and inclusiveness.

If square lines and neat layout stand for virtue, dignity and restraint, then the graceful *ruyi*-shaped cloud design (a mushroom-like decorative motif symbolizing the fulfillment of wishes) on the chair back, the sensational *chiffon* lampshade and the soft design of the vase represent gentleness and charm. The rich personality of people and objects here reveal themselves.

A big Chinese-style painting table is used as a Western dining table and arranged in a Western style. Two different types of chairs are on each side of the table, identifying both the host and the guests. A piece of colorful fabric, which appears as if fresh from a weaving machine, becomes a unique Western table cloth. A mirror with European frame reflects down on the recessed-leg table. The selection of furniture and accessories is ingenious, bridging Chinese and Western culture.

Brick carving is a unique art commonly used in traditional Chinese architecture. Thanks to years of refinement it has been perfected, and through the carving numerous stories and good wishes are related. Having a whole piece of a brick-carved door as a wall decoration is a unique addition to a room. This approach, which utilizes exterior design in interior design, adds style, and together with the furniture and accessories creates a truly classic atmosphere.

BEDROOM

The Chinese regard the bed to be a very important piece of furniture. In old times, when a daughter of a rich family was getting married, the family would select the best timber and find the best carpenter to make a perfect bed for her. So, choosing a large bed embellished with carvings is a smart shortcut to a Chinese-style bedroom. The red canopy adds a festive element to the room and makes the bed a private space in the small room.

The canopy bed is the definite focal point of this room. The corner with a pouch table and a round chair plays a good supporting role. In addition to having a rest, you can also work or groom yourself in this room.

Strictly speaking, the furniture is more representative of a Southeast Asian style, but the design has a strong Chinese flavor. Is it the red wall, the pair of melon lamps, the red hot water bottle, and the porcelain crock? Or is it because items on the shelf were once believed as required in marriage? Chinese style is so strong that even incorporating just a small amount will affect the feeling of a room.

Red used in a bedroom not only adds a feeling of warmth, but also echoes the Chinese theme. The Chinese calligraphy patterns bring a sense of freshness and elegance. The bed headboard uses modern materials with Chinese patterns. And its shape is reminiscent of the moon gate.

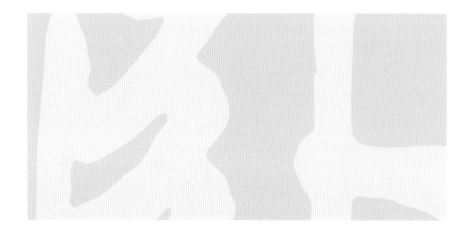

Layers of *chiffon* curtain are used to section off the area occupied by the canopy bed and to soften the raw feeling of the wood. The wooden box with carvings substitutes for a bed end bench. It is Chinese-style furniture in a Western layout.

The room showcases the traditional Chinese spirit in its every item, from the canopy bed, table, noodle cabinet, vase, vessel, right through to the tea set. Notably, the small cabinet beside the windows is covered with soft cushions, becoming a corner for you to have a rest. It feels like both a Western lounge sofa and a Chinese beauty's chair, and is a bright spot in the room.

This modern bed has arc-shaped legs, an outward curving apron and a square board, in line with traditional shapes. The three pieces of art hanging above the bed give new meaning to tradition by their modern composition. The stand with carvings, though low-key, nails the overall style of the room with its authentic and classic design.

The classic symmetrical layout plays a defining role in this room, along with other important specifics. The two old chests used as bed end benches reflect the blend of Chinese and Western cultures, while the items displayed on them are authentically Chinese. The painting deliberately placed on the left side of the bed seems to find a balance between two cultures.

In this black-and-white setting, a Chinese touch is apparent in the reflection of the lights in the mirror and stainless steel. The frosty-looking bamboo branches convey a feeling of purity and pride; the seemingly lonely embroidered coat is elegant and charming. The puppet on the bed cabinet adds drama to the room. The mirror on the wardrobe door is also of unique design. All these elements of Chinese style underline the theme.

STUDY

Some pieces of modern furniture in this study do not compromise the classic elegance: The no-frills, long, narrow desk is reminiscent of an old narrow rectangular table with corner legs. The bookshelf has been simplified and is just made up of several wood boards, but its classic grain and color are still there. The stylish floor lamp is equipped with a lampshade made of traditional materials. The entire design is kept as simple as possible to leave room for the imagination.

One characteristic of classicism is its refinement and attention to detail in both craftsmanship and planning: a classic study design should have a couplet on which your motto and name is written. When the selection of paper, Chinese ink, writing brushes and ink stones is carefully thought out, the arrangement of the furniture will only add to the adornment of the room.

A study with a comfortable chair to sit on and windows that allow sufficient sunlight in is where you can really get into your books. A set of classically elegant furniture, a bouquet of wispy lilies and a peaceful-looking Buddha statue will aid you in your relaxation.

The furniture in the study looks classic, but its low-profile tones are in sharp contrast to the brightness of the overall design; its square look goes well with the straightforwardness of the decoration, making the overall image quite fashionable. Thus the modern office appliances, like the printer, are able to fit naturally into the setting. This study achieves perfection in both design and functionality.

Antique collections are displayed in the cabinet here, itself an antique. The profound darkness is balanced out by the red wall. The overhead adjustable trajectory lights highlight the collections from perfected angles. The modern, industrialized look of the lights stands out in exception to the classic study, enriching the diversity of the decoration.

The decoration in this study is as simple as a snow cave—enabling the user to concentrate on reading. Those who choose to sit on a hard wooden chair and read in front of a simple desk in today's impatient world must be persevering and hard working, enjoying their own company. Maybe the old *qin* instrument (similar to a zither) on the wall is waiting for its soul mate to come, perhaps likewise with its owner.

KITCHEN & BATHROOM

The overall style of this room is as simple as a piece of white *xuan* paper (Chinese painting paper); it is in the extras that the style of the room is revealed. Behind the glass door lies a half screen. The bluestone on the ground shows the tranquility of China's south area of the lower reach of the Yangtze River after rain. The blue and white porcelain vessels on the side of the bathtub are charming—with or without flowers in them. The picture "of lotus rising out of water" on the drapery has profound meaning, even though it might not be the expected flower for the moment.

The mosaic-covered wall hides the water pipe underneath it. But what matters more is that it sets perfectly well off the old style washstand. The dressing table is more modern, and the openwork carved vase is used as a chic table lamp base.

On the left is a commode transformed from antique carved furniture; on the right is a freestanding bathtub with gold, claw-shaped legs. On the east side there are cloisonné hand-washing bowls with dragon and phoenix patterns on them. On the west side lies an exotic carpet. Here you can find light concealed in the Chinese-style lampshades; there you can find sunlight filtering through the Western-style white shutters. The old, the new, the foreign, and the Chinese are interwoven and mutually reinforcing.

This photo is very interesting. There are two planks with opening section; one hung vertically, the other horizontally. It seems that they are in very close proximity, but in actuality the mirror is used in such a way so as to make the two opposing walls seem next to each other. This approach is derived from the traditional method reflecting faraway scenery. In addition, the red color widely used functions well as a transition between fashion and tradition, and achieves passionate and reserving feelings at the same time.

If a blue-and-white bowl is used as a sink to wash hands in, then the accompanying cabinet must be ancient enough to be equally elegant. If you think of the blue glass on the wall as a quiet lake, the niche in the wall as rough mountain rocks, you will suddenly find you are in nature. The fastidious and low-profile Chinese know how to hide poetry and imagination in their daily life.

The ground is covered by bluestones in the shape of the Chinese character *ren* (人, people), whereas the mosaic on the wall has the auspicious pattern of a dragon and a phoenix. Although it is an old bronze basin that is put on the equally old, yet classic washstand, it is equipped with a water tap and mirror to meet the needs of modern life. The traditional table and the cane-covered stool both play their roles well enough to satisfy people's daily needs.

The moon-like mirror acts as a foil to the silver willow twigs, offering a poetic touch. The exquisite black wood basket, red silk scarf and red felt carpet are like the stamens of a plum blossom, embellishing and tempering the brightness emanating from the moon-like mirror.

The red square bricks on the surface of the bar counter become the focal point amongst the light coloring of the room. They also inject Chinese flavor into a typical western setting. The curtain is made of strings of beads and stainless steel. The combination of ancient and modern styles as well as the use of different materials is fresh and unique. The wooden handle on the glass door, the colorful pottery on the table and the unadorned chairs all embody Chinese characteristics implicitly.

OTHERS

Sometimes it feels good to sit on the ground, just as our ancestors did, because you may discover something new in the mundane when viewing from a different perspective. You can take a moment to live your life like your ancestors: to read books or look at the clouds, to drink tea and enjoy tranquility. It seems that life can be better savored only when you would slow down your pace. If you are in the mood to play, even the chessboard under the sunshine exudes poetry.

The climate of Northern China is very cold. Therefore, people try to do everything possible on the warm *kang*, whether entertaining a guest, eating, resting, or sleeping—you name it. That is why the *kang* gradually came to be the most important piece of furniture in the people's lives. In this case, you will notice that the rose-red cushion and the delicate accessories and appliances complement the simple, unadorned *kang*-shaped furniture well. The gauze curtain creates a secluded, ethereal environment for relaxation. Finally, the skylight brings the natural transition of changing sunlight and moonlight into the room.

A true tea lover knows how to appreciate tea leaves, savor the aroma, watch the change of the water's color and finally savor the drink. From tea things, the way you make the tea, to the ritual of drinking tea, the whole process is refined. Then a proper environment is all essential. Light tea is the most subtle variety, and the drinking environment should be the same: no excessive decoration. A plain tea table and a set of no-frills stools are enough. The only thing that matches the grace of the tea lover is the bamboo on the wall.

The stone sculpture only occupies a tiny part of the space, but its flavor permeates the room. The huge low-profile abstract picture echoes well with the sense of the ancient given off by the sculpture. The wall is covered by white stones, their rough surface fits perfectly with the atmosphere. In the far corner there are traditional Chinese chairs and a table, waiting for something to happen.

Chinese elements are skillfully used to fit into this elegant and fashionable decorating environment. The narrow rectangular table with its corner legs has retained its simplicity by doing away with unnecessary details. Antique vases have been replaced by two symmetrically arranged crystal table lamps. Mirror stands have been replaced by no-frills frames. The delicate motif on the door clearly defines the classic flavor of the space.

There are no flowers in the vase on the flat-top recessed-leg table, but the poetry on the horizontal inscribed board is as beautiful. The thought of "meaning matters more than words" is one feature of traditional Chinese decorating. The red musical instrument resonates with the coloring of the table and the board. The old door shut behind with the similar color to the floor adds a sense of mystery into the space.

This space is very picturesque. Small things from different eras are scattered about, expressing the beauty of humanity and nostalgia. The nostalgia emits from the glaze of the bottles and the bamboo steamer, or even the aroma of the orchids.

The sofa bed (the three-side paneled bed), which in old times was used to accommodate guests, is now a place to display antiques that date from such times. The old wooden case with a table lamp on serves well as a narrow *kang* table. The crocks that carried water are now accessories. Maybe tomorrow they will become vases...

Traditional Chinese furniture is about pragmatism and simplicity. But that does not mean it is not beautiful: The *ruyi*-shaped cloud lock on the case is beautiful, the teapot shaped space that the chair legs create is beautiful, the red paint is beautiful, and the chic drawer is beautiful. It is the details that make the everyday items from the old days into immortal art.

The ladder shaped twin coffer table harmonizes with the abstract painting, whereas the clay sculpture is balanced visually by the table lamp. It appears as if the round stool aside and the fan on the table bring inconsistency. But it is such casualness that blends art with daily life, making a man-made scenery more natural.

The delicate half table and the stone can been seen from one direction; the bamboo screen and the pictures on it can be seen from another. So whether heading upstairs or downstairs, you will always see something beautiful. The limited space is full of delicate and elegant Chinese characteristics: bamboo, stone, the wooden gnarled floor and the pebbles where the floor meets the wall. All are understated, colored natural things.

This layout is a vivid example of how the concept of an "axis" is used in traditional Chinese decorating; when looking from the doorway, you will find that the major pieces of furniture are all on the same axis. It can be said that this balance brings a certain solemnity to the space. The door is the frame with the best angle to show off the design. The view outside the glass door, the most beautiful backdrop of the framed "picture", adds another dimension to the space.

Sometimes a redundant place, thoughtfully designed, can be the highlight of your home. In this case, cabinets, with their changing colors and materials, are arranged at different heights, making the corner of the stairs a unique place for exhibition. Sometimes you don't need excessive decoration, because emptiness itself makes a statement. The umbrella, the thin branch, and the handrail on the stairs are all the epitome of classic.

There are scores of items on exhibit on the deck cabinet alongside the wall, which is a natural extension of the traditional feeling the bamboo door gives off. The two windows connect and slightly reveal what is inside the drawing room. The highlight, perhaps, is the paper umbrella in the corner; you may just take a glance at it unintentionally, or you will take it in as you depart. Either way, it adds a little surprise and excitement to the room.

The multi-drawer cabinet has an ancient Chinese flavor, whereas the picture on the wall is completely Western and modern. However, the two coexist peacefully and generate a feeling of eternal youth. The armored boot on the cabinet reveals that the owner loves and esteems Chinese opera and traditional art. The straw-woven basket in the corner has a dual identity: as an exhibit, and as an appliance, bringing people back from the fantasy of art to everyday life.

Whether it is the flower pattern in the center of the floor, the furniture, the decoration on the wall, or the lights, the uniformity of color tells clearly the Chinese characteristics of the space. The carefully made recessed-leg table with everted flanges and the delicate fan strike a comfortable balance, further highlighting the theme of harmony. The miniature mountain stone and the arranged flowers in the vase, both on the right side, have been balanced out by the larger empty space on the left.

You can see a Buddha statue and incense burner on the recessed-leg table. The step in front of the table signals a shift of space. The place where Buddha is worshiped should be higher than the rest of the room. The orange cushions in front of the step and the coquettish pink picture on the wall have added a bit of warmth into the scene.

The screen here has multiple functions. In this case, it divides space; it's a backdrop for the exhibits on the table, a decoration in itself. The red color of the gauze curtain adds a Chinese flavor, and its semi-transparency creates a sense of haziness, a very typical Chinese feature.

If only you had this kind of a corner—one with glorious flowers in spring, delicious fruit in autumn; singing birds and the scent of flowers; the beauty and grace of the Master chair (the straight-backed wooden armchair) and the tenderness of silk. Here, even the beautiful view outside the windows cannot distract you. The carved windows can close and serve as a backdrop, adding another piece of charm into this wonderful space.

The two armchairs with curved armrests are on the same side of the recessed-leg painting table. This seemingly odd layout actually expresses casualness and liveliness. The old *xibao*s (bulletins of glad tidings) have fashionable frames, and the Chinese characters appear more like artwork. From this we see that the familiar and traditional elements of life, if put together in the right manner, have surprising freshness.

If you look carefully, you may find that the lower end of this noodle cabinet is wider than its higher end. Such uniquely shaped Chinese furniture usually stands alone, and its outstanding coloring makes it the focal point of the room. The scattered melon lamp, delicately arranged flowers, bamboo blind, stone sculpture and pottery around it create a natural and relaxed atmosphere in the living room.

This Master-like folding chair of the Song dynasty was the original look of Master chairs (the straight-backed wooden armchair). However this chair is rare with its straight headrest and the lengthened body. What is even rarer is the fact that it is now used as a writing table, on which the candle resonates with the shining gourd lamp. The two writings on the wall—half past and half present—best exemplify the time-transcending harmony of the space.

The furniture in the corner is full of life. The multi-drawered cabinet, the wooden stool and the round case are mottled through many years of use, giving them a practicality that contradicts their use as an ornament. They are daily appliances, products of the old days, the charm of which reveals the taste of the homeowner.

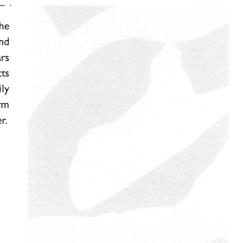

This small space is divided into three parts by two doors. This is a traditional way of dividing space in China: glass, which divides space but does not block sunlight, and wooden doors, which accomplish both those tasks. With one door closed and another open, the space feels reconnected and interwoven. You first see the blue and white porcelain, then the bronze beast-headed door knockers. The design draws your interest to know what lies beyond, in the view outside the windows.

The unadorned brick wall brings an element of history into this space. The elegant wooden window allows sunshine in to break the silence. A typical miniature tree sits squarely on the carved cabinet. Such subtle but telling Chinese characteristics turn an otherwise boring corridor into an unforgettable place of unique personality.

The Chinese style gate provides a strong and clear line between what is inside and what is outside, and meanwhile highlights the style. Looking through the red-painted gate, there is a screen that blocks your view. This aspect is one vital feature of traditional Chinese buildings: The zigzag path is what leads to the hidden tranquility. The space between the gate and the screen acts like a transition that sends out a clear message: you are now at home.

The classic openwork window and the modern style glass railings strengthen the connection between the different parts of this space. What is more, they draw one in to try harder, in an effort to see more. But the openwork window is decoratively superior: The beautiful pattern and the top-notch craftsmanship always satisfy—whether there is a beautiful view outside the window or not.

The elegant shape and refined craftsmanship make the cage itself a piece of art. Its huge size and central positioning causes one to contemplate its profound meaning: the world outside the cage, the bluestones, the shadow of the tree... Isn't it a refreshing world?

Imagery is a vital part of traditional Chinese art. The cage, green wall and green leaves are associated with a quiet and artistic garden. The ordinary cane chair entices you with the thought of stealing a half day's relaxation out of your busy life. The view outside the window makes you dream of the singing of birds and the scent of flowers...

CHAPTER TWO ADDING CHINESE ELEMENTS TO YOUR HOME

Not every design lends itself to showcasing a complete Chinese style. However, even a table, a cabinet, an accessory or a color can impart a little Chinese flavor.

For example, blue-and-white porcelain reflects the elegance and grace of the Chinese style; a red lantern gives off warmth and joy. Ming furniture is about refinement and simplicity; wooden cases and wooden *kang* tables are about grandness in simplicity. Using color reflects prosperity and bustle; black and white are about purity and serenity. China's rich history and diverse culture gives us a lot of options. When decorating your home, choose the most appropriate elements that fit in with your existing decoration, thus expressing the unique features of China.

Buying some traditional Chinese furniture is one wise option. This could be a Master chair, a recessed-leg table with everted flanges, a sofa bed or a canopy bed, you name it. With careful thought, any traditional furniture or unused space can play a vital role in defining the decorating style of your home.

Another wise choice is having accessories with Chinese characteristics. These could be anything from china or jade ware to stone or wooden sculptures. An ancient style openwork flower board instead of some average pictures will certainly win admiring glances; brocade cushions evoke a Chinese flavor more than cushions made from the usual fabrics. As long as you choose your accessories carefully and wisely even modern, simple decorating can be very Chinese.

Another choice is to create different moods by changing the color. The traditional Chinese color schemes are quite interesting: red and green are lush, red and pink are coquettish, yellow and purple are regal. What is more, the red of China is world renowned, blue and green are elegant and low-profile, and not to be overlooked is bright yellow, at one time exclusively used by royals. It is not necessary to purchase new things all the time; appropriate use of color also gives off a Chinese flavor.

So, the right decorative elements, be they furniture, accessories or combinations of colors, will make your home like a gift in wrapping; once you open the door, you will find the mysterious and permeating uniqueness of the Chinese flavor unveiled.

FURNITURE

The beautiful tree on the wall is reminiscent of Rococo style, which often focuses on using plants for decorative purposes. You will also discover branches and leaves laid out on the Chinese open-shelf cabinet and the sofa bed. Those familiar with Rococo style are aware that it is related to the Qing style in some aspects, and this scene vividly illustrates the connection.

The figure and color of this Master chair indicates solemnity and extravagance. The equally old big painting table is simple and unadorned. The porcelain folding screen with traditional Chinese painting appears simple, perhaps, but has profound historical meanings. This depth balances out the differences between the screen, the table and the chair. Thus the entire space looks bright and elegant.

Screens are one of the oldest types of furniture in China. Putting one in a simple, modern space will instantly evoke a Chinese flavor. The trajectory lights enhance the carving and its pattern, making it vivid and lively. Even the resulting shadow on the wall looks like a traditional Chinese painting.

The folding chair is the most important type of chair in China. In fact, it is a symbol of power and because of this fetches high prices at furniture auctions. The traditional folding chair is very convenient because it can become compact for storage. However, it is not very stable, because the weight is borne at the point where the legs of the chair cross. The round backed folding chair in this picture has been modified by adding two poles, ensuring even weight distribution. This modification fortunately does not compromise the overall simplicity and elegance of the chair.

This space has multiple colors and rich decorative elements. The wooden Chinese cases and cabinets echo the naturalness of the sofa and fabrics, with their warm colors being a natural fit with the equally warm environment. Furthermore, the cases and the cabinets' beautiful patterns and fine details highlight the theme of the space: a sense of decoration and design.

A Chinese element can find its place even in the warmth of Mediterranean style decorating: the red painted deck cabinet is a natural fit in this lively environment. Other details, like the dark colored locks and handles are of great historical and cultural significance. A piece of Chinese furniture also makes the place more exotic.

If you try it you will know that the simple yet comfortable Chinese armchair with its backrest lives up to its centuries-long international reputation: the armrests cradle your arms; the curved back contours to your back perfectly. Maybe that's why Ming dynasty furniture has maintained its worldwide popularity.

The furniture of the Ming dynasty, like this Yoke backed armchair, focuses on simple and smooth figures, whereas the furniture of the Qing dynasty, like this carved window, is delicate and extravagant in style. That is the diversity and moniker of traditional Chinese decorating. On the one hand, it is warm and gregarious, like the red brocade; on the other, it is cool and striking, as exemplified by the vase and the Buddha statue.

The designer creatively uses metallic paint to decorate the traditional carved doors, and the shine of the color further highlights the shapes and the patterns of the carving. The effect adds a modern footnote to its traditional elegance, and a supplement to the overall effect. Besides, the openwork carving is of practical significance: It ensures sufficient ventilation for the cabinet.

The delicacy of the Chinese style is found in details here: the comb back of the chair, slightly curved, supports the back of the one sitting in it; the double-ring pattern in the middle of the handrail is auspiciously Chinese, and it adds softness to the square and hard chair. What is more, the details of the table and the pattern of the window are all reminiscent of the eternal pursuit of delicacy and excellence.

This wooden square tea table has a soft bamboo top, which offsets its heaviness and adds a diversity of materials. The bamboo is an effective enhancement that adds detail and keeps the overall look simple. The traditional flower table in the corner is also kept as simple as possible to complement the modern style furniture. The classic colors and patterns echo the classic style.

One common way of bringing history into a room is to use an old case as a tea table. However, a little more uncommon and clever way to do it is to use a piece of simple and unadorned blue cloth with a white flower pattern as a tablecloth, adding a touch of the natural. This gives a feeling that the designer has a deep understanding of how to use traditional accessories.

Although the sofa bed has lost its original function, it is still a place for leisure and relaxation in today's world. You can sink into the soft cushions and silk pillows; you can enjoy tea and snacks on the *kang* table; you can read, chat with friends or just close your eyes and rest. Whatever you do, it is a place to relax and enjoy.

The unadorned wooden folding screen has helped give a place for tranquility and elegance. Its natural grain is in sharp contrast to the glossy surface of the lighted table. Furthermore, it is a unique backdrop for the ornaments and accessories on the table. Its free and easy style sets the tone for the bright and elegant space.

The reading table is unique amongst all the traditional tables because of its smooth and elegant look. It is relatively low, and is usually placed on the *kang*. The divan sofa was the most prestigious place to sit in ancient times. This sofa bed is made with impeccable craftsmanship and design, and is an expression of the owner's hospitality. Nowadays, some classic furniture has lost its original function, but one can now instead focus more on the artistic and decorative attributes of such pieces. With proper accessories, the furniture becomes a piece of art in the room.

Warm colors and patterns are a symbol of honest and unsophisticated traditional Chinese customs, whereas the delicate lock and the bronze sheet decoration is an expression of traditional Chinese craftsmanship. The room looks a little bit dark and hard, but the nostalgic cabinet door offsets that feeling to some extent, and the familiar patterns make people feel warm.

The simple design and the deep purple color give new life to a traditional Chinese Canopy bed. The soft and transparent purple gauze screen complements the hard furniture, making the entire room feel full of love and romance. There are two pillows and two moon-shaped lamps. Everything is in two's—it is a room for couples.

If not for the Chinese writing table, this scene would lose its present temperament completely. The table's extravagance ensures that the surrounding environment is elegantly simple. The craftsmanship of the table causes the rest of the furnishings to look natural, and not mediocre. Interestingly, their beauty comes from different ends of the world; the European style table lamp base goes perfectly well with the Chinese style writing table.

Beds in China were once superior to stools and chairs. Beds have many forms in China. One example is the *kang*, still found now in northern China; another is the *ta* which is the long and narrow couch, arrayed with pillows, as displayed in the picture; the sofa bed is the three-side-paneled bed displayed on the *kang* screen. Here the *ta* is not only a place to sit on, but also the core of the setting, because it is centered by the *kang* table, the *kang* screen, the silk, and the famous painting. All these elements give a strong Chinese flavor.

A row of deck cabinets, the old style locks and bronze sheet accessories have defined it: this space is about traditional style. The deck cabinets are very practical—they are big enough to hold a television set, a DVD player, a sound amplifier and numerous compact discs. The famous 1930s Shanghai beauty calendar in the picture frame has brought poetry into the room.

It is said that Wang Anshi (a great politician and thinker) of the Song dynasty invented the Double-*xi* (囍, happiness) pattern by putting two *xi* (喜, happiness) characters together because he got first place in the national exam and got married at the same time. This shelf copies the famous auspicious element of Double-*xi*. The Chinese red and metallic grey, when put together, highlight a three-dimensional fashionable style, whereas modern materials and design express age-old best wishes.

Gold is a common color in traditional Chinese decorating. Here a typical piece of the Qing dynasty furniture—the red painted case with gold pictures on it—is a case in point. In this instance, three cases are stacked together, and the Buddha statue on top of them looks like it is sitting suspended in the air. This is an ideal example of the look that can be achieved when using traditional elements in a fashionable way.

Judging by the depth of the bed, it likely originates from the late Qing dynasty, and it is a sofa bed-turned Opium bed. The gilt edged pattern on the panels of the bed is a symbol of the decorative Qing style, whereas the small European style accessories in the corner give evidence that Chinese furniture of that time was gradually influenced by the western style. Times change, functions change. But what does not change is that a dainty and charming bed always wins people's attention.

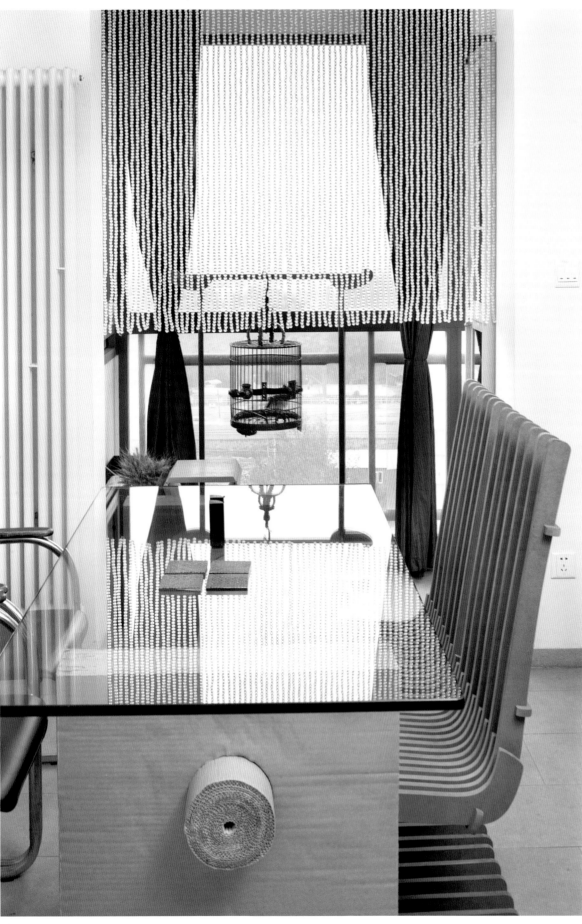

The chairs look simple and natural, and the subtle width change on the sides is what the designer wants to make an impression on you: like the flowing beauty of Chinese calligraphy. Furthermore, the plywood-like chairs have a strong sequential beauty, and the table paired with them is also very different: it's pleasing in appearance, but what is more amazing is that it is made of paper board!

These pieces of modern furniture and accessories have taken traditional elements and reorganized them. The narrow rectangular table has a unique grain due to the wood it is constructed from. The wooden rack sitting behind the table could be a clothing rack, a towel rack or a lamp rack. Either way, what really has effect is its simple look. Such modern designs can still be classic and historical precisely because of their deep cultural roots.

The dark color of this bedside cabinet highlights its charming and delicate patterns. Its classic extravagance gives a focal point to this scene. If you look carefully you can discern the connection between the Qing style and the Rococo style; they both use botanical patterns and soft, zigzag lines to embellish. What is different is that Qing furniture is usually made from heavy and rough materials, giving a more solemn look than the light-and-exquisite materials used in European furniture.

Sometimes we are just accepting of the fact that old pieces of furniture, seemingly of no use in modern life, are nothing more than artwork. When, in fact, we can make them useful again by changing their roles. Take this washstand as an example, instead of putting a bronze basin on it for hand washing, you can put a porcelain bowl on it to hold fruit, or next time, orchids. The delicate carving on the towel rack and the aroma of the orchid are both classically elegant.

Bamboo gives a feeling of refreshment, and thus is widely used to make furniture in the warm and humid south. The gnarls on the cabinet are highly decorative and are a statement to the owner's dignity and integrity. The cabinet looks simple and unique due to the unique pattern the bamboo creates. The effect is that even classic furniture looks modern and fashionable.

The traditional washstand and tub were two of the most common daily use items in old times. Years later, they again find their place in daily life and become an artistic exhibit. Beauty transcends time and is hidden in the simple and unadorned appearance of this piece with its age-old, rough veins. This piece sits in stoic confidence, with the weight of history behind it.

The master chair in this drawing room is quite interesting; it is wide and deep, but with relatively short armrests. It is a chair for meditation, where the one seated crosses his or her legs to meditate. Here, the wooden meditation chair looks plain, simple and elegant, inviting people to sit on it to see beyond the world of mortals. The nearby lamp has a paper cover and three thin branches as its support. The chair, the lamp, and other pieces of furniture make the space feel natural and unpolished.

The red stools on the left side of the picture have been balanced out by the red palace lamp on the right. The symmetrically distributed pottery bottles on the table lend a sense of stability. The classic ladder-shaped cabinet has unique veins and adds bright color. Its half-ancient-half-modern look has brought vitality into this nostalgia, making it the center of the space.

The unique ladder shaped table on the right side of the picture can be divided into two types, depending on the number of drawers: a twin coffer table and a triplet coffer table. This type of Chinese furniture functions both as a table and as a cabinet. Its functionality is why it is so popular in the West. With an equally classic and elegant armchair on the left side, and a miniature tree on the top, the table tells you immediately what Chinese style means.

This pink-wall-blue-stone combination is clean and clear, and the furniture is modest. The gilt-edged pattern on the red painted cabinet has faded over the years, but it has gained a sense of certainty and relaxation. This echoes perfectly well with the lively flavor of the red woven baskets on top of the cabinet and the food basket in the corner.

The sofa bed, the gilt-edged cabinet, the red painted plate, the dragon patterned carpet, all give a wonderful glimpse of China. The dragon pattern, which was once exclusively reserved for the royal family, is now found in ordinary people's homes. The *ta* bed, on which people used to cross their legs and sit, now becomes a fashionable sofa. The dowry case is now used as a tea table. Things change, but the beauty of art is enduring.

The cute, dainty and charming cabinet and the slim and delicate clothes rack both have a feminine flavor, and the open dressing case on top of the cabinet even allows for a scent of rouge and powder. Such pieces of furniture are so impressive that one can be almost certain that this is a room for women, even if you see no flowers or silk.

A narrow *kang* table is usually put on the *kang*. Thus, its name. A narrow *kang* table is a relatively short type of furniture, eliminating the need for everted flanges to prevent things from falling off. Because of this, the *kang* table usually looks round and cute, as is the case with the one in this picture. Its *ruyi*-shaped cloud Medallion is the highlight of the overall softness and cultural heritage.

This chair is made by today's technology, but it takes into consideration the essence of Ming dynasty furniture and thus expresses a Chinese flavor. The Chinese table series created by the famous Denmark furniture designer, Hans Wegner, has many such chair styles. In fact, furniture from Scandinavia uses natural materials, puts people first and advocates traditional beauty. This has much in common with the simple and delicate Ming dynasty furniture.

Screens have many functions in traditional Chinese decoration. For example, one is usually placed behind the seat of honor on important occasions, and is a symbol of power and force. In this case, the eight-fan folding screen is a powerful support to the chairs in front of it. Moreover, its huge size, excellent craftsmanship and unique color make it the focal point of the scene.

Our lifestyle and habits change all the time. As a result, many pieces of furniture have lost their original functions. For example, in the past, clothes were laid out on a clothes rack, not hung on it. Here, the clever designer makes a little modification and restores the clothes hanger's functionality. Its classic and elegant look is a nice visual contribution, and its function space-saving.

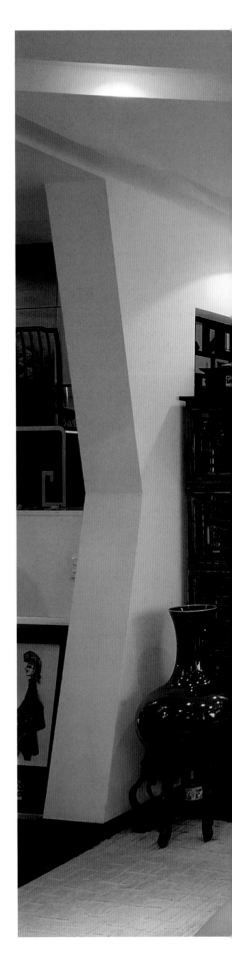

You don't have to worry that a mainly European decorating theme will be in conflict with delicate Qing dynasty furniture. History books tell us that Rococo style was influenced by the Qing style; they were developing around the same time. They both focus on decoration and slim silhouettes; both value delicate, complex and refined craftsmanship. Even a common element of the Rococo style, the "beast leg", has been used in this piece of Chinese furniture.

The miniature tree is one unique form of Chinese art that traces its roots all the way back to the Tang dynasty. The miniature tree primarily focuses attention on the window view, but maintains a harmony between the scenery, the basin and the table. The recessed-leg table with everted flanges has been modernized and simplified, but its dark color and grand figure still have the essence of traditional Chinese furniture. What is more, its low key look means it plays a qualified supporting role to the solemn and elegant leading star, the pine.

Traditional Chinese furniture is the highlight of this black and white picture: the classic elegance goes well with the modern simplicity; the traditional steadfastness complements the modernity. Looking closer, you can see that the armrest of the chair echoes the curve of the wall. The distance between them is the distance between now and then, black and white.

ACCESSORIES

The tea table seems to be made of a Xi'an stele. The cushion material seems to have been taken from a cheongsam. The strokes characteristic of a traditional Chinese painting on the wall are very graceful. The painting is hung obliquely and in doing so conveys a trace of irreverence. The owner of the apartment must be an interesting woman who is consumed by painting, calligraphy and literature.

Composition is very important. The roots of an ordinary poplar, placed in the right way on a bamboo stand in a simple displaying case, becomes imposing and grand under the right spotlight. The twisting shape and coarse exterior represent the silent cry of a tenacious life.

The sparse plum blossoms in the vase convey Chinese tranquility and calm. The number of accessories has been sacrificed, but this photo shows that sometimes less is more. Of course, there are countless beautiful accessories available, but only a select few are suitable to the atmosphere of a room, and able to express the character of the owner.

The decorative stone is regarded as a mute poem and a three-dimensional painting, and since ancient times has been deeply favored by Chinese people of letters and refined tastes. Placing such stones in a room is a traditional form of decorating. The thin, hollow, shining and contorted statue in the photo is set off by bamboo shoots, and appears especially elegant and unworldly.

One usually doesn't imagine a stone horse statue and a bronze camel statue to be decoratively compatible. But thanks to the designer's ingenious arrangement here, the two objects are presented in a way that conveys a sense of humor. Arranging very traditional artifacts in a creative way is a very modern approach that creates a very unusual effect. There are tiny Chinese characters written on the surface of the cupboard. This post-modern approach breathes fashion into traditional culture.

If there is only a mottled old table in the room, it is going to be simple and humble. However, in this scene, a red lunch box with a handle features on the wooden windowsill. Thus, the room feels rustic and natural. Sometimes, the right accessories are like a charming expression in a person's eyes, instantly lending character to an ordinary face.

Using simple bricks to offset a Buddha statue is very ingenious. The composition of the bricks and the way they are laid is very much in harmony with the atmosphere of simplicity and originality. The simple process of baking bricks gives a feeling of Zen. After all, it is only after going through raging flames that mud can be transformed into solid brick. The very process seems to reiterate that it is only through forbearance that can one be a true Buddhist.

Just for a cushion with the pattern of white-and-blue porcelain on it, the western cloth sofa can have the sheen of jade. Only a latticed plank enables the simple white curtain beside reveals just enough luring grace. The Chinese style is so distinct here, that only a glimpse can tell it.

If accessories have genders, then the lamp on the wall is a Chinese woman, owing to the crimson color and full lines. On the other hand, the erected partition with refined texture reminds one of a handsome and learned young man. The gentleness created by the cream-colored wallpaper and the combination of accessories make the room a place where romantic stories seem to take place.

After contemplation, can you find something common among the seemingly very different items, ceramic statue, porcelain vase and lamp here? Their shapes are in some ways very similar. It is not only in the West that the beauty of the human body is worshipped. The lines of traditional Chinese works of art also implicitly reflect appreciation for the human body.

By appreciating this ceramic jar one can come to understand a lot about China. The simple material of the jar reflects the pursuit of nature. On the other hand, its refined patterns show the attention paid to decoration. The smoothness reminds one of gentleness and flexibility. Its heaviness and steadiness breathe solemnity and grandeur.

These colored statues are very vivid and lively. The skilled carving of their clothes is exquisite. The statues have great artistic value. Interestingly, they are very small compared with the furniture next to them. Placing such fine and unconventionally small objects in the corner is a very impressive approach.

Judging from the shapes of the stone statues, they derive from very ancient beginnings. In arranging the positions of the statues, the designer illuminates them with slanting light, and in doing so, highlights the coarseness of their surface and the glory of their history. Light shines through the mottled shadows of plants and leaves on the wall, creating a wonderful backdrop for the statues.

This set is used to make traditional pastries. The small and finely carved set of tools is indicative of the leisurely lifestyle and constant pursuit of refinement possessed by the people of ancient times. The box in the back is made up of three sections. When a handle is attached to it, the box can be used to carry food conveniently. Such tools are no longer used now. The box, with its unsophisticated shape and function, is a very unique item.

The oil lamp with traces of black soot and the bright handmade doll are pieces of folk art that represent the simplicity and unsophistication of the northern rural Chinese people. The dolls are in the likeness of domestic animals. There is an exaggeration in pattern and use of rich color that shows the designer's appreciation for enjoying a beautiful life. What is most interesting is that the designer arranges all these dolls on a rough plank. The coarseness is very much in harmony with the character of the dolls.

China's Dragon Boat Festival is also called "Five Poisons Day," the day on which demons appear. On this day, people in ancient times would wear a sachet which was supposed to exorcize evil spirits. Today, this legendary tale has almost been forgotten, but the sachet is still popular as a traditional artwork. It can be used as a decoration. Its fine workmanship and herbal fragrance permeate a home with a scent of Chinese tradition.

The old-fashioned thermos bottle is used as a vase. Although there are no flowers on twigs, the festive colors and gorgeous patterns remind one of blooming flowers, and speaks the happiness loudly. The abstract painting on the right looks quite modern and cool, and contrasts well with the bottle. Still, they echo each other because they are both bright in color. This corner of the room feels very warm and cozy in the flickering candlelight.

The look of the lamp here is both modern and classic. The two wooden poles are similar to a lamp designed by Sapper, the German designer. However, the lamp also has the look of a hand-held lantern as used in ancient times in China. The material and shape of the lampshade is similar to traditional court lamps. The warm orange light complements the purple curtain, bringing a touch of luxury and brightness to the elegance of the room.

The central focus of the scene here is "double happiness," the two Chinese characters. On the red pillow, they dominate, taking up the center of the pillow. On crimson ones, they are intertwined, with their lines artfully arranged. What's more, the two characters can be altered somewhat and are hidden in the pattern of the board. Their implications are reiterated by the blossoming peonies, the embodiment of wealth in Chinese tradition.

There are some parallels here between the instrument, which looks like an ancient book, and the bamboo leaves. The smoothness of the instrument softens the harshness felt in the squareness of the room. The two pieces of roof tile represent ancient culture and history. They are in sharp contrast with the modern measuring instrument. This contrast adds liveliness to the otherwise commonplace room and gives an impression of time travel.

This pot is actually not hollow; the flowers are painted on the wall. However, one still get the illusion that lotus leaves were dancing in the wind and the tender lotuses were blooming emitting refreshing charms. We can surmise that the owner of this apartment is an elegant and virtuous person.

What is interesting is that although the objects on the table are different in shape and material, they are all containers. A Chinese character with the meaning "good fortune" is embedded in the hexagonal window. Perhaps the owner is praying for good fortune. Decorating with this slant—one that includes expressions of good wishes in such a implicit way—is typically Chinese.

The Chinese styled stone gate decorated with steel cranes on either side is similar to the scene picked up from neighborhood's courtyard. The large stone sculpture depicts a courtyard. The narrow long table implies that these are indoor objects. Although the table holds nothing, it conveys a lot of meaning on the aspect of space.

The wood and the bamboo curtain, along with the green leaves and the light, all supplement each other and give a feeling of coolness and quietness. The focus of the scene is the melon-shaped lamp with its green gauze shade. Light penetrates the gauze and casts a faint light over the entire room. Even the lamp stand and flower table seem to be covered by years of moss in the green light. The fern leaf bamboo, the lamp and the curtain each factor in, creating an ascending and descending degree of green with a poetic touch.

A Buddhist statue is always awe-inspiring, beautiful and worthy for worship, whether it appears in a painting or in sculpture form. The smooth lines and carving display the beauty, grace and placidity of the Buddha. The elaborate drawings and carvings are meticulous.

The elephant is one of many auspicious animals of Chinese tradition. The pronunciation of "elephant" in Chinese is very similar to that of "auspiciousness." One conveys their wishes for good fortune when they place an elephant-shaped ornament in their home. Also, elephants can drink a large amount of water which is a metaphor for wealth. Therefore, elephant ornaments are regarded as symbols of prosperity. This stone sculpture is done in a classical style and looks smooth, full and graceful. It is a delicate work of art.

This is a very interesting ornament consisting of a statue of an elderly gentleman and pieces from a real chess set. This combination of an unreal person and some real chess pieces feels very natural and lively. It inspires in one the desire to refrain from disturbing, and, rather, to silently observe the game.

Buddhist statues have more than just religious significance; they are also sculptures with artistic value. This Buddha has full and streamlined contours. He looks peaceful and solemn, and the trail of benignant smile is discernable. The spiraled hair and bun look neat, orderly and vivid. As a Buddha statue is no ordinary handiwork, it always soothes and placates especially in the lights of candles.

Here, the simple symmetry is reminiscent of a young and virtuous girl from a rich family. The porcelain, kylin (Chinese unicorn), and table screen are skillfully made and contribute a feeling of decency. They are like the smile or knitted brow of a traditional girl who always conforms to etiquette.

The four planks with open sections are an inspirational touch. The rich and classic silk and satin bedding at the end of the bed complements the classic feel of the planks. How appropriate that there are two pillows on the bed, each embroidered with flowers that are symbols of love and happy marriage.

The bamboo in the frosted-glass light box feels different from the live plants that are usually used as accessories. The bamboos create a vague haziness. This arrangement gives the feeling that the bamboo is wavering outside the window. The bamboo also accentuates the Chinese style and offsets the porcelain, earthenware statuettes, and imperial jade seal.

Porcelain is synonymous with China. White-and-blue porcelain embodies the spirit of traditional Chinese paintings in their simplicity, and has been popular ever since it was invented. This style is the type of porcelain that has the most distinctive of Chinese features. This porcelain is set out in such a way that that it provokes one's thoughts and expresses deep, enduring meaning.

The etchings of flowers and birds on the vase and the dragon shape of its handles have the very distinct character of traditional Chinese art. The material the vase is made from and the shape of its mouth is of a more Western style. This combination of Chinese and Western styles gives a striking visual impression of prosperity and abundance. In contrast, the stone Buddha and the white-and-blue porcelain jugs are simple in color and shape, giving an impression of unworldliness.

As early as the mid-seventeenth century, Chinese style was popular in Europe. In the eighteenth century, the style became intertwined with Rococo. The chinaware in this photo represents the integration of Eastern and Western art. The base and mouth showcase the refined carving skill of Europe. The lid and body embody the Chinese crafts of porcelain. The two styles set off and complement each other.

From the plethora of lattice, to the uneven grain of the wall and the tidy patterns in the sofa and carpet, you can find trails of traditional Chinese realistic painting. The porcelain vase on the wooden table boasts a beautiful sheen and smoothness and is the focus of the scene. The loose and close layouts transit freely yet naturally. Set off by the rough wall and refined lattices which are made with an exquisite touch, the vase appears very grand.

In this photo, almost everything evokes a feeling of tradition. There is the color red, symbolic of China. There is a double-happiness symbol, which is seen all over China. There is half a lotus leaf, as in a traditional Chinese painting. There are also classic traditional patterns. All these elements are different, but have strong Chinese characteristics in common.

In the spirit of traditional Chinese culture, one should conform to nature and find harmony with it. The wooden table, mat and cushion are all made of natural materials. The shapes of the wooden plate and pottery were arrived at through inspirations from nature. Traditional Chinese art both reveres and leverages natural things in an attempt to achieve the ultimate harmony between man and nature.

The wooden boxes on the table are extremely simplified, with only color and shape. The stone statue next to them is very exquisitely carved to details of the facial expression, body and clothing. They are totally different objects, but are connected by the black pedestal, which achieves something common between the two. Moreover, the concrete and abstract patterns on the door co-exist in harmony, being made of the same simple and natural material.

The door with its carved patterns and the exquisitely made table set off the Buddhist statute. This setting does not make one feel lonely and unworldly, but rather, content and placid. The stools on either side of the table inject more vitality into the scene.

Accessories can not only indicate one's appreciation of beauty, but also one's status. Here, the two calligraphic works are used as two partitions in a fashion way. This novel practice strikes visitors, and implies the good breeding and refine taste of the host/hostess. On the table there are only a few accessories, but their artistic value shows that their owner's interest.

Red lanterns are one traditional accessory that has probably the strongest Chinese flavor. Its festive color and fullness embody people's desire for a good life. The color of the lantern-shaped lamp balances that of the plant and paper umbrella in the distance. The happy and auspicious lantern softens the heaviness of the Chinese-style cabinet.

Some accessories are essential and indispensable. Others add grace to beauty and bring perfection. The accessories in this photo belong to the first category. Without the touch of maroon, there might be too much solitude and quietness in the room. Without the couplet hung on the wall, there might not be a gracefulness in the space. What is most amazing is that the accessories and overall style of the room are in perfect harmony. The silk brocaded cushion is elegant but not loud. The dark-colored frame is simple, yet solemn.

Porcelain and glass. Chinese painting and European-style furniture. These contrasts are unexpected, but quite workable. A home is not only about looking beautiful. It is more about being comfortable. Before thinking about style, one might as well pay more attention to practical matters like the function and comfort of the room. A good design can strike a perfect balance.

In China, many popular poems attach deep cultural meanings to various objects. For example, bamboo, which stands upright, has nodes and is hardy, thus implying integrity, perseverance, and freedom from material pursuits.

The sofa with piping, the bright and colorful patterns on the pillow and the glass base of the lamp all smack of the modernity of Shanghai in 1930s. The contrariness of that modernity has been abandoned, and what is left is truly classical. Just look at the plaque: Although having experienced vicissitudes, made of ebony and handsomely etched with smooth, handwritten gold characters, it is still appreciated and relished by later generations.

The beauty of this window with its open sections is in its moderation. The graceful curves and exquisite workmanship are unforgettably beautiful, and complement the wonderful scenery outside.

Traditionally, fancy doorknockers were only found on the door of well-to-do households in China. A doorknocker for an ordinary household was very simple. Interestingly, this pair of doorknockers with its copper animal faces could only be used by royal families. The glaring eyes of the animals and the countless nails look both intimidating and awe-inspiring. Thus the belief that they could exorcise evil spirits.

In the art of decorating in the Chinese tradition, the circle and square represent the sky and earth, respectively. From this partition, one can see how things are arranged in leading and supporting roles. Moreover, in traditional art, things are expressed in extremely detailed and abstract ways, and integrated into one work of art. In this partition, there are detailed depictions of hair, wrinkles and simplistic straight lines. The two extremes balance and complement each other.

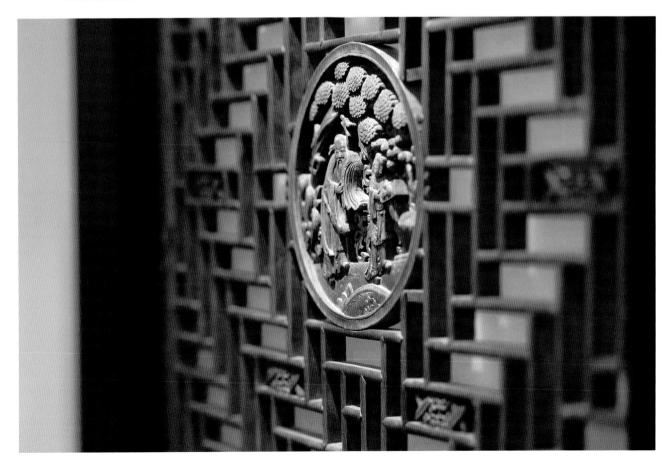

Thanks to the delicately arranged accessories, in this room one seems to hear birds singing and smell the fragrance of flowers. The branches of the bonsai reach into the birdcage. It's such a lively landscape; the birds may begin to chirrup at any moment. The branches lean slantingly in the vase against the backdrop of the latticed screen, one can almost smell the faint aroma of plums.

Here we see two round objects. One is modern and simple, the other classical and splendid. One is as fluid as water, the other as strong as a rock. One is innocent, the other sophisticated and profound. These are the differences between the East and the West, and between art and science. Because of these sharp contrasts, the features of each are more pronounced. Their juxtaposition enriches the effect of the accessories.

In ancient times, the candle was the main means of illumination. The candlestick was a daily appliance. However, today, apart from holding a candle, the candlestick alone can also be used as a decoration. This candlestick with simple lines complements the modern style well due to its novel material. But its classical colors and symbolic look still convey traces of Chinese tradition.

In a Chinese apartment one will often find vases and a mirror stand placed on a table near the door. Here, two vases are placed on either side of the stand. On the wall, there is a big mirror. The symmetry provides beauty of order, and preserves classical conceptions of space.

In the midst of modern and refined accessories, it may seem abrupt to place a wooden Chinese style door in the room. The designer brings in an avant-guard unframed glass door to carry the overall fashionable style. The wooden door painted black gives a Chinese feeling, and the copper animal-shaped doorknocker further strengthens the traditional feel.

The curtains in the reflection of the mirror convey romantic feelings. The sofa bed is charming in itself, and the silk fabrics make it more exotic. The sunlight is softened by the curtains. The half-dark and half-bright atmosphere of the room is brimming with gentleness and tenderness, allowing one to forget the passage of time.

Sometimes, appropriate accessories can not only embellish a room, but also be the soul of the room. They can upgrade simplicity to refinement, and cleanness to purity. The lighted wooden Buddhist statue in the photo lends conciseness and unworldliness to the space around it, thanks to its natural material, primitive shape and smooth outline.

In this colorful world, adhering to the simplest colors, black and white, persistently, needs a lot of skills. In this corner, many materials are used: stone, glass and aluminum alloy. There are accessories made of leather, silk and cotton. Although only two colors are used, thanks to the variety of materials and textures, there is not an overall feeling of dullness. Instead, the room leaves an impression of delicacy and refinement.

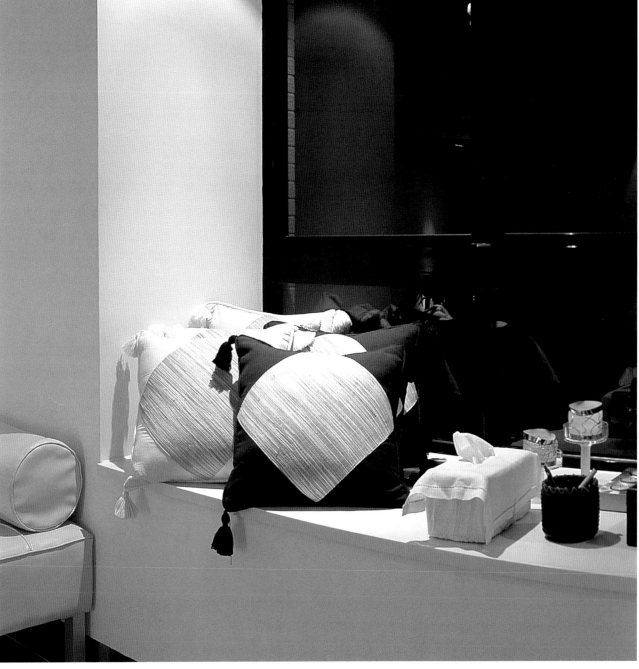

COLOR

The moment the mirror door is opened, a ray of light goes into the otherwise blue and gray-toned room. The red wall sets off the white toilet contrastively. The gilt frame brings more charm to the accessories. There is a Chinese romanticism in the surprisingly dazzling beauty. This is like a traditional Chinese woman dressed in black clothes, seemingly reserved and solemn, but secretly exposing her hidden pink lining in the wind.

The ocean of blue in this room, in perfect harmony with the delicate Chinese furniture and accessories, is like the colors of classic white-and-blue porcelain, cloisonné and other traditional handiwork. The room has a rich classical atmosphere. At the same time, the multi-colored carpet warms up the room and thereby counteracts the effect of the dominant and sometimes impersonal cool colors. The colors in the carpet are compatible with the main color scheme and bring vividness to the room.

The grass green wall, natural-looking root and down-to-ground openwork screen with the cracked ice pattern make one feel as if this room were a quiet and secluded study. The scarlet curtain falls to the ground at the moon gate. Its color is in sharp contrast to the dominant color of the room, making one feel as if the room is a boudoir.

The combination of blue bricks and antique furniture makes this room heavy with history. However, the red doors with carved patterns give the room a feeling of modernity, as the doors seem traditional but are able to transcend the boundaries of tradition. The red color is not only in line with traditional concepts regarding beauty, but also brings harmony to the traditional furniture and the modern pendants.

The reddish orange of the main wall, the vermillion of the cushions, and the color of the cupboard are very similar. The warmth of the red-based tones makes the room feel cozy and genial. Another important aspect of the room here is the floor, which is covered with a blue and purple carpet, complementing the wall color. In this way the bright colors are toned down and the colors in the pattern are able to echo the dominant colors in the room.

The flaming passion of the red carpet flows like a stream, but is abruptly checked by the black sofa. The clash of the two strong colors grabs everyone's attention. Unexpectedly, the color of the curtain is quite in harmony with the red. The mystique and elegance of the curtain blends the sharp contrast of the two colors.

An ordinary earthen jar, when wrapped in red yarn, becomes more classical in style. An abstract painting with only grains on it becomes representative of Chinese style when done in red. Red has become the quintessential symbol of China.

The wall is yellowish green, a traditional Chinese color. This color is a great contrast to the pink color of the cushions. Together, they create a feeling of beauty and delicacy. In the monumental literary work *The Dream of Red Mansions*, this same match of colors is mentioned. The curtain and wooden couch are black and white, respectively, and as the purest colors, they set off and temper the brightness of the room.

The warm orange color on the wall echoes the intimacy of wooden furniture. At the same time, fashionable colors are used together with the traditional furniture, to create a sharp contrast and complement. The light blue used in some areas separates the room into different sections and also grounds the axis on which one table and two chairs are sitting. This separation highlights a decorating style that is both traditional and classical.

The wall painted cobalt-blue, a cool color, is in direct contrast with the warm-colored furniture. The bright yellow, fuchsia and grass green of the carpet and cushions add to the variety of color. The black sofa in the corner is not eye-catching, but brings a welcome feeling of stability.

The luxurious red velvet curtain and the classic red table are like frames with several accessories at the center. The gold foil wallpaper, the golden decorative paintings and the draping of red combine to create an atmosphere of royal grandeur.

With the aid of refined red accessories, the room becomes gentle and charming. The red screen with patterns of birds and phoenixes is exquisitely made. It bodes good fortune and showcases graceful artistry. The red silk cushions are black in the middle, adding variety in color and stability in vision. In the vast sea of red, the plantain plants in the corners of the room bring a poetic touch with the combination of green and red.

Scarlet and bright yellow have significant meaning in traditional concepts of beauty in China. They used to be monopolized by the royal family, and today they are the colors of China's national flag. Red represents festivity and auspiciousness. Yellow represents brightness and strength. In the room, the combination of the scarlet brocaded sofa and yellow calligraphic works is gorgeous and splendid, bringing a sense of happiness and energy.

The red of the wall is the focus of the room thanks to its bright color. It occupies the central position and highlights the symmetry in the layout of the table, chairs and accessories. Although the tradition of hanging a board or decorative painting along the axis of the room has not been followed, the use of Chinese red follows through and keeps tradition alive here.

Against the backdrop which is framed in white, the red sofa, tea table, lampshade and decorative glass all add a sense of a cozy home, and enhance the festive atmosphere, characteristic of Chinese style. They are like a painting in which red plum blossoms are placed in vast area of white snow.

Without these two red embroidered cushions, the bamboo curtain in this black and white environment would be elegant but lonely. However, with the added red accessories, the Chinese style of the room is highlighted and the entire living room becomes overwhelmed with warmth, festivity and joy.

The entire wall here is painted red. Thanks to the distinctive features of the wall, there is a sense of refinement. Slight tonal changes in the red give special light effects, and make the room feel multi-dimensional. In certain parts of the wall, there is openwork carving. Its classical Chinese style echoes the dominant color and improves the overall impression. Moreover, the several green leaves moderate the abundance of crimson and further strengthen the visual impression.

The traditional red wall is the backdrop to the classic-style table and the melon-shaped lamp. The color of the wall echoes the modern painting. Red, being both classic and modern, links the seemingly different furniture and accessories very naturally, achieving multi-element decorating effect.

The silver-gray tempers the boisterousness brought about by the red and gives an anchoring feeling of modernity. Silk is used to display and develop the traditional Chinese style. It also serves to echo the refined and graceful shiny texture of the silver gray. In this manner, fashion is injected into the room.

Red is definitely the dominant color of this room, but it appears in different textures. The overwhelming feeling is one of festivity. The red gives such a strong impression that the black of the furniture and the white overhead are affected, and become a mere extension of the red.

Set off by the dark colored wall, the red sofa is especially eye-catching. The red lantern and its tissue paper echo the sofa in color. The cushions, made of brocade, match the sofa in spirit, and accentuate its Chinese style. The green-toned painting on the wall and the fish tank do not take away from the red. Rather, they complement and underline the festive warmth of the red.

People of letters and refined tastes in ancient times often used dark green to express their unworldly character and high-flying aspirations. This was in direct contrast to the more popular use of red, which was used to represent good fortune. Even their beloved bamboo, landscape paintings, bronze and collections of ancient jade were a shade of green. The vast green in this room brings a sense of seclusion to the rustic furniture, and also fully conveys the virtue of the owner.

The combination of green mosaic filed wall and the glass door of the shower brings coolness to this space. On the cupboard, the china bowl with its patterns of flowers and birds is more like a piece of art than an implement used for washing. The pattern of red flowers on the bowl is set against a green background, echoing a line from a poem that reads: "a spot of red in a vastness of green."

Mauve is a very delicate color. It is neither stiff nor loud, and wonderfully injects a sense of reserve into glamour. In this space, the graceful silk is done in this poetic color. A fine string grasps the silk curtain, obscuring the view of the room somewhat. It is clear that the designer is very familiar with the traditional Chinese decorating concept of not revealing all. This way, people's curiosity to know what lays inside is aroused.